SWIFT SUCCESS GUIDES™

I'M BUYING MY FIRST HOME. NOW WHAT?

A Roadmap from First Search to Closing Day

BRIDGET McCREA

STRONGTIDE PRESS

ISBN: 979-8-9946587-6-5

First Edition

Published by StrongTide Press

www.strongtidepress.com

Printed and distributed in the United States of America

Part of the StrongTide Press First-Time Homebuyer Series

Swift Success Guides™

This book is for informational and educational purposes only. The author is not an attorney, accountant, tax professional, mortgage lender or financial advisor. This book does not provide legal, tax, mortgage, financial or other professional advice. Laws, rules, lending standards and requirements change. Every situation is different, so please consult a qualified professional for guidance specific to you.

Any products, services, URLs or organizations mentioned are included for reference only. The author has no affiliation with them and does not endorse them unless specifically stated. Use your own judgment before acting on any information in this book.

STRONGTIDE press

CONTENTS

Let's Bring the Pressure Down Before You Buy.....1

How to Use This Book.....5

CHAPTER 1: The "Am I Ready?" Homebuyer Checkpoint.....9

CHAPTER 2: Don't Let the Lender Pick Your Number.....23

CHAPTER 3: What the Lender Will Want from You.....37

CHAPTER 4: Buy a Home That Fits Your Life.....51

CHAPTER 5: Look Beyond the Listing Photos.....65

CHAPTER 6: Before You Commit to the House.....81

CHAPTER 7: Stay on Top of Inspections, Title & Disclosures.....93

CHAPTER 8: Walk into Closing Prepared, Walk Out a Homeowner.....107

Keep This Book Handy Until the Keys Are Yours.....119

Get Your Free Homebuyer Toolkit.....121

Pay It Forward for the Buyer Starting Where You Did.....123

Build On What You've Learned Here.....125

About the Author.....127

StrongTide Press Books.....129

LET'S BRING THE PRESSURE DOWN BEFORE YOU BUY

Buying a home is exciting, but it can also feel like too much all at once. You're making expensive decisions, signing legal documents and trying to keep your head straight while everyone around you seems to need "one more thing."

Since I wrote the first edition of *The Homebuyer's Question & Answer Book* in 2005, things have definitely gotten more challenging for first-time buyers. So much so that going through this full book update felt a lot like opening a time capsule. Buyers today are dealing with a very different market:

- Home values have hit record highs in many U.S. markets.
- Housing inventory is tight, so there are fewer available homes to choose from.
- Online house hunting helps until every search gives you too many homes, a lot of different opinions and a lot of reasons to second-guess yourself.

- Getting a mortgage is more expensive, thanks to higher interest rates and other unavoidable factors.
- Recent real estate commission changes mean buyers need to know more about agent agreements, compensation and which fees they might have to cover themselves.
- Insurance and property taxes can be harder to predict and budget for.
- Most lenders expect high credit scores, clean paperwork and more cash upfront.

Unfortunately, home prices, borrowing costs and other expenses have risen faster than paychecks. That leaves many first-time buyers trying to absorb larger monthly payments and one unexpected expense after another without stretching their budgets too far. The fact that you picked up this book means you're already doing what smart buyers do: checking the numbers, watching for problems and giving yourself time to make good decisions.

This book takes the same core guidance from *The Homebuyer's Question & Answer Book* and breaks it into sections you can use when you need them, whether you're comparing homes, talking to a lender, reviewing an inspection report or trying to figure out what happens next. Every checklist, reality check, question and warning sign in the pages ahead will help you navigate the process. The info is easy to share with a partner or pull up on your phone before a showing, lender call or second look at a home you're thinking about making an offer on.

You can jump to the chapter that matches wherever you are right now, run through the relevant lists and move on. If you're still figuring out whether you're ready to buy, start with Chapter One. If you're already under contract and trying to keep track of everything before closing, go straight to Chapters Seven and Eight. This book meets you wherever you are in the process, from the initial Redfin search to setting up a homeowner filing system.

I've also been in your shoes recently. I bought my last home two years ago as a self-employed, divorced woman with no co-borrower. That combination can send mortgage underwriters running for the hills, trust me. I know what it feels like when the process starts moving fast, stalls out or hits a snag that makes you wonder if the whole deal is about to fall apart. I also know what it feels like to wait on paperwork, worry about the approval, watch the numbers change and wonder if you're missing something important. I know what it takes to get to the closing table, and I want to help you get there too.

Ready to do this? Let's jump in.

HOW TO USE THIS BOOK

Think of this book as a decision-support tool for the homebuying process. Each chapter uses the same six-part format, so you always know what's coming next and can jump to exactly what you need. Here's how each section is set up.

Smart Buyer Checklists

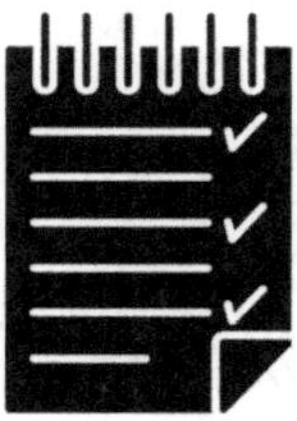

These are your pre-flight checks. Before you move from one step to the next, run through the relevant checklist to make sure you haven't missed anything important. The Chapter Two monthly payment checklist, for example, walks you through every cost in your housing budget (not just the mortgage payment). The document prep checklist in Chapter Three outlines exactly what your lender will ask for, so you're not scrambling when you see the doc request in your portal.

Reality Checks

Here's where you'll pause, think through decisions and make sure you're not getting pushed by fear, outside opinions or excitement. The Chapter One Reality Check asks whether you're buying for the right reasons or because other people think you should. The one in Chapter Six helps you decide whether your offer price makes sense based on recent sales or whether you're getting carried away because you love the house.

Questions to Ask

Use these when you talk to lenders, agents, inspectors, sellers, attorneys or anyone else involved in the process. The questions align with the conversations buyers typically have at every stage, from lender calls and second showings to inspections, title issues and closing. Pull up the right list before the conversation starts and you'll have the questions you need right at your fingertips.

Warning Signs to Watch For

These are the issues first-time buyers miss when they're overwhelmed, excited or just trying to keep the deal on track. Some are obvious once you know what to look for and others are easy to excuse away when you really want the house (or just want the whole process over with already). Use them to catch problems before you make an offer, sign something or agree to terms you don't fully understand.

Next Steps

Each section ends with a few specific things to do next, like calling a lender, finding a document, asking your agent a question or checking a figure before you continue. Use them to keep small questions from turning into expensive mistakes later.

At the end of each chapter, you'll also find five questions and space to reflect on what you learned, what needs to be confirmed and what new questions to ask.

1

THE "AM I READY?" HOMEBUYER CHECKPOINT

Smart Buyer Checklist: My Real Reasons for Buying

How many of these sound familiar? You may be tired of renting, ready for more space or done living by someone else's rules. Before the buying process really gets started, take a minute to think about why you want to buy and what you want from your next home.

- ☐ Tired of helping someone else pay off their mortgage every month.
- ☐ Ready to stop moving every time a lease is up.
- ☐ Starting a family and need more space.
- ☐ Relocating for work and want something stable instead of another temporary rental.
- ☐ Sick of sharing a wall, ceiling, floor or common areas with neighbors.
- ☐ In a long-term relationship and this is the next step we both want to take.
- ☐ Want to be able to paint, renovate, improve or make the place mine.
- ☐ Ready to start building a financial asset that can appreciate over time.
- ☐ Have the down payment saved, credit in reasonable shape and feel financially ready.

- ☐ Need a dedicated home office, or space for your startup business or side hustle.
- ☐ Can buy a place for about what I'm already paying in rent each month.
- ☐ Want a place that's completely mine to share with a pet the landlord never allowed.
- ☐ Job is stable, income is steady and staying put for a few years makes sense.
- ☐ Want to build equity instead of watching rent payments disappear every month.
- ☐ Ready to stop feeling like a guest in someone else's property.
- ☐ Want a yard, a garage, more storage or outdoor space that rentals don't always offer.
- ☐ Tired of waiting for someone else to fix things that should have been repaired months ago.
- ☐ Ready to put down real roots in a neighborhood instead of just passing through it.
- ☐ Want the tax benefits that come with owning instead of renting.
- ☐ Buying makes more financial sense than renting in today's market.

Reality Check

Am I Really Ready or Am I Just Reacting?

Buying because it makes sense for you is different from buying because everyone else is doing it. This checklist will help you figure out whether you're prepared for homeownership or reacting to FOMO, impatience or someone else's expectations. Check off the statements that apply to you, then look closely at any you left blank before you start talking with lenders or looking at homes.

- ☐ My timeline is mine, and it's not being determined by family, friends or anyone else.
- ☐ I know owning isn't like renting. There's no landlord to text when the HVAC stops working at 9 p.m. on a Sunday night.
- ☐ My job is stable and I'm not expecting a major life change in the next year or two.
- ☐ I'm not buying because everyone around me is doing it and I don't want to fall behind.
- ☐ I haven't been watching too much HGTV and convincing myself this is easier than it is.
- ☐ I understand that "hot market" panic is a thing, but so is buying a house before I'm ready.

- [ ] I've thought about what happens if something goes wrong in year one and I have a plan for dealing with it.
- [ ] I'm not already looking for the exit before I've even made an offer.
- [ ] I can say yes to this with confidence, not just "I guess I'm ready."
- [ ] I've run my actual monthly numbers (not just a ballpark), and the payment fits my real life.

Questions to Ask First

Ask Your Lender

- ☐ Is this a good time for someone in my financial situation to buy? (A lender can explain the loan side, but you decide if the payment and timing work for you.)
- ☐ What would prevent me from getting approved right now?
- ☐ What credit score do I need to qualify?
- ☐ How much money should I have saved before I apply for a mortgage?
- ☐ What's the difference between what I can borrow and what I can comfortably afford?

Ask Your Real Estate Agent

- ☐ What does the market look like right now for first-time buyers in my price range?
- ☐ How long are homes sitting before they sell?
- ☐ Is this a good time to buy or would waiting make a difference?
- ☐ What do most first-time buyers underestimate going in?
- ☐ What else should I know before we start looking at homes?

Ask Yourself

- ☐ Am I taking this step because I want to or because I feel like I should?
- ☐ If this turns out to be more expensive than I expected, what's my backup plan?

Warning Signs to Watch For: Before You Buy

⃠ **You're doing this because you're sick of your landlord.** Owning means no more rent increases or ignored repair requests, but it also means every repair bill and maintenance job becomes your responsibility. Make sure there's more driving this decision than just frustration.

⃠ **Your job, location or life plans could look completely different in a year.** A new job, relocation or breakup could force you to sell much sooner than planned. In some cases, the cost to sell and move again can wipe out any money you made on the house.

⃠ **You haven't sat down and done the math yet.** The mortgage payment is only the starting point. Property taxes, insurance, maintenance and repairs can add hundreds of dollars to your monthly cost, so be sure to factor them in.

⃠ **You're not sure what you can spend on housing every month.** If you don't have a handle on your current spending, it's hard to know how a mortgage payment will impact it.

⃠ **Someone or something outside your own life is making this feel urgent.** If everyone around you is more excited about this than you are, that's a sign to pause and make sure the timing, money and responsibility still make sense for you.

Next Steps: Get Your Foundation in Place

Before you start touring homes or talking numbers with a lender, take a hard look at the decision you're about to make. Know why you want to buy, what you can comfortably pay each month and how you'll handle repairs, maintenance and surprise bills after closing. Those answers will tell you whether you're ready to buy or if waiting, saving more and staying put makes more sense.

Start With the "Why"

- Know why you want to buy now.
- Make sure the decision goes beyond just being tired of renting.
- Don't let a lease deadline, rent increase or bad landlord rush you into buying.
- Buy when it works for your life, not when family, friends, social media or other buyers think you should.
- Think about whether you expect to keep the same job and stay in the same area for the next few years.

Get the Money Side Ready

- Know your monthly income, bills and regular expenses before you start talking purchase price.
- Look at the payment you can live with, not just the number you may qualify for.
- Remember that the mortgage payment is only one part of owning a home.

- ☞ Build taxes, insurance, repairs and maintenance into your total payment calculation.
- ☞ Think through how you'd pay for the first major repair, whether it's the HVAC, water heater, roof or plumbing.

Know What You're Taking On

- ☞ Understand that owning isn't just like renting with a different payment; it's a whole other level of responsibility.
- ☞ Plan for repairs, maintenance and surprise costs before they happen.
- ☞ Make sure your job, income and location can support this step.
- ☞ Look past the closing table and think about your first year in the house.
- ☞ Make sure you want the responsibility that comes with the keys.

5 Questions Before You Move On

The homebuying process starts moving quickly once lenders, real estate agents, sellers and inspectors get involved. Use these questions to pause for a minute and think through the steps you've already taken, what still needs attention and any questions you should ask before taking the next step.

If you're reading the paperback, jot your answers in the space below or in a notebook you're keeping for the buying process. Got the ebook? Open a notes app or doc, take your notes and save them for later.

1) What do I know now that makes me feel more prepared than I was before?

2) What should I double-check right now before taking the next step?

3) What question do I need to ask my lender, agent, inspector, attorney or other professional?

4) What number, document, deadline or detail is keeping me up at night, and why?

5) What one thing should I confirm right now before moving on?

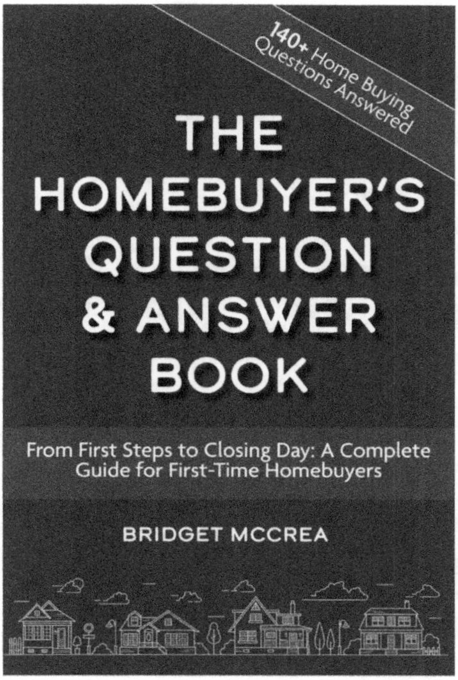

Need All the Answers in One Place?

If you're already in the thick of the homebuying process and feel like you need the full picture in one place, *The Homebuyer's Question & Answer Book* has everything covered from start to closing day. It's the anchor book in this First-Time Homebuyer Series and an excellent resource to have on hand if your situation is more complicated or moving faster than you expected.

2

DON'T LET THE LENDER PICK YOUR NUMBER

Smart Buyer Checklist: What You'll Really Pay Every Month

A lender, website or app will give you an estimated loan amount, but you still have to decide what payment works for you in real life. The number a lender quotes and the one that hits your bank account every month may be two different things. Make sure you know the difference before you start shopping. Use this checklist to get a picture of your full monthly cost before you start looking at homes in a specific price range.

- ☐ Your principal and interest payment, which is the base mortgage number you'll see quoted most often.
- ☐ Property taxes, estimated by your lender but often reassessed after closing at the home's new sale price (which can push the number higher in year two, so be aware of that).
- ☐ Homeowners insurance, required by most lenders and can be a major addition to your payment depending on the home, location and coverage needed.
- ☐ Private mortgage insurance (PMI) if your down payment is under 20%. Your lender will tell you the monthly cost and when you can ask to have it removed, usually after your loan balance falls to 80% of the home's original value.
- ☐ Homeowners association (HOA) fees if the home is in a community that has one. These vary widely, so check the fee, what it covers and how often it can change.

- [ ] Flood insurance if the property is situated in a FEMA-designated flood zone. This is a separate policy from homeowners insurance.

- [ ] Utilities: electric, gas, water, Wi-Fi, cable and trash. You'll be paying for them yourself unless you're buying a condo or townhouse, where some of these services are built into the HOA fee.

- [ ] Lawn care, snow removal or exterior maintenance that a landlord used to handle and that you'll be taking care of yourself.

- [ ] A monthly maintenance reserve. A widely used rule of thumb is to set aside 1% of the purchase price per year for repairs. On a $400,000 home, that's $4,000 annually or about $333 per month.

18-Point Payment Reality Check

You may qualify for the payment, but that doesn't mean it fits your monthly budget. To be safe, run that number against your bills, savings, everyday spending and the first major post-closing home repair.

1. My take-home pay covers the payment without depending on overtime.
2. I can pay my regular monthly bills without shuffling money between accounts or making any late payments.
3. I'll still have enough for groceries, gas, insurance, childcare, healthcare, pets and other everyday expenses.
4. I can keep adding to my savings after I buy.
5. I'll have money in the bank after paying the down payment and closing costs.
6. I won't dread seeing my mortgage payment come out of my account every month.
7. I won't have to cut every Friday night dinner out, weekend trip or small extra from my budget.
8. I could handle a car repair, veterinary bill or medical expense without missing the mortgage payment.
9. I'm not counting on a raise, bonus, tax refund or side income to cover the payment.

10. I don't have to become a completely different spender to make the numbers work.
11. I could handle a reasonable increase in property taxes, homeowners insurance or utility bills.
12. I've included HOA dues in the monthly total, if the home has them.
13. I could pay for an early repair, such as a broken water heater or HVAC problem, without depleting my savings.
14. I won't spend every dollar I have just to get through closing.
15. I picked the payment based on my budget, not the maximum amount the lender approved.
16. I'm not raising my budget because other buyers are spending more.
17. I know where the money will come from each month. I'm not telling myself I'll figure it out later.
18. I can make the payment and still have money left for the rest of my life.

Questions to Ask First

Ask Your Lender

- ☐ What's my full PITI payment, not just principal and interest?
- ☐ How did you estimate taxes and insurance?
- ☐ What's my cash-to-close number?
- ☐ When can I drop mortgage insurance and what triggers that?

Ask Your Attorney (if you're working with one)

- ☐ What's your fee and when is it due?
- ☐ Are there any title issues I should know about before we get to closing?
- ☐ What do I need to bring to the closing table?
- ☐ Is there anything in this contract I should push back on before I sign?

Ask Your Real Estate Agent

- ☐ Are there HOA fees in the areas I'm considering?
- ☐ Is asking for seller-paid closing costs realistic in this market?
- ☐ What do buyers in my price range underestimate most about upfront costs?

Ask Yourself

- ☐ Can I comfortably make this payment every month, or am I just taking the lender's word that I can afford it?
- ☐ Am I comparing this payment to my rent, or to my full monthly budget?
- ☐ If something breaks in the first six months, how will I cover the repair cost?

Warning Signs to Watch For: When the Numbers Don't Add Up

- ⃠ **Basing your decision solely on the principal and interest number.** Include property taxes, insurance and mortgage insurance in that total.
- ⃠ **Calculating affordability on gross income.** Use take-home pay instead because that's the money you have left after taxes, insurance and other payroll deductions.
- ⃠ **Savings will be zero after closing.** Year one of homeownership always comes with costs you didn't see coming, so be sure to set some cash aside for this.
- ⃠ **Haven't asked for the cash-to-close number.** Get the estimate early so you know how much more you need to save.
- ⃠ **Counting on a raise or bonus to make this work.** Base your budget on what you earn now, not money you may or may not get later.
- ⃠ **HOA fees aren't in the budget.** These fees are mandatory and may even increase over time, so be sure to factor them in.

- ⃠ **Buying at the top of your loan approval range.** Qualifying for a loan and affording it aren't the same thing, especially once you add in taxes, insurance, repairs and the rest of your monthly bills.
- ⃠ **Haven't thought through a job loss or income drop.** Run through that scenario a few times before you commit.
- ⃠ **Planning to renovate right after closing without budgeting for it.** Major renovations aren't cheap, and that money has to come from somewhere.
- ⃠ **Haven't run this through an actual monthly budget.** A calculator can give you a number and your budget tells you if you can live with it.

Next Steps:
Start Thinking About Closing Costs Early

It's never too early to start thinking about how much cash you'll need to bring to the closing table. Plan for 2% to 6% of the purchase price. On a $450,000 home, that's going fall between $9,000 and $27,000, which averages out at $18,000. Your lender must give you a Loan Estimate within three business days of your application, and that'll include a more accurate number.

Every deal is different, but here are some of the main costs you'll see on it.

- ☞ Loan origination fee
- ☞ Title search and title insurance
- ☞ Attorney fees (required in some states)
- ☞ Recording fees
- ☞ Prepaid interest through the end of the closing month
- ☞ Homeowners insurance (often collected at closing to cover the first full year)
- ☞ Property tax escrow to fund your account
- ☞ HOA dues, if applicable
- ☞ Transfer taxes, in some states

5 Questions Before You Move On

1) What do I know now that makes me feel more prepared than I was before?

2) What should I double-check right now before taking the next step?

3) What question do I need to ask my lender, agent, inspector, attorney or other professional?

4) What number, document, deadline or detail is keeping me up at night, and why?

____

____

____

____

____

____

5) What one thing should I confirm right now before moving on?

____

____

____

____

____

____

You're two chapters in, which means you already know more than most buyers do when they start this process. If that's true, please say so in a quick Amazon review. Even a sentence or two can help the next buyer find this book when they need it.

3

WHAT THE LENDER WILL WANT FROM YOU

Smart Buyer Checklist: Mortgage Document Prep

Start gathering these documents before you make an offer. Some may take time to track down, and your lender will need them to verify your income, assets and financial history.

Proof of Income

- ☐ Pay stubs from the most recent two months
- ☐ W-2 forms for the last two years
- ☐ Tax returns for the last two years
- ☐ 1099 forms for contract, gig or freelance work
- ☐ Profit and loss statements or business tax returns if you're self-employed
- ☐ Social Security award letter if you receive benefits
- ☐ Documentation of other income like alimony, child support or gig work

Asset Statements

- ☐ Checking and savings account statements from the last two to three months
- ☐ Retirement account statements
- ☐ Investment account statements
- ☐ Certificates of deposit, bonds or business accounts (if applicable)

Other Documents You May Need

- ☐ Photo ID
- ☐ Social Security card or ITIN
- ☐ Copy of the ratified sales contract once you have it
- ☐ Proof of rent payments or a copy of your lease
- ☐ Gift letter if a family member is helping with your down payment
- ☐ Business license if you're self-employed
- ☐ Divorce decree or bankruptcy documents if applicable
- ☐ Employer names and addresses for the past two years
- ☐ Residential addresses for the past two years

Reality Check

Prequalification vs. Preapproval

These two words sound alike, but they're not the same thing. This will help you understand the difference before you start making offers.

- Prequalification gives you a rough estimate based on basic information you provide. It's a starting point, not a commitment.
- Preapproval goes deeper and means the lender reviewed your income, credit and financial documents.
- Many sellers won't take you seriously without a preapproval letter.
- Preapproval tells you how much you can borrow, your estimated monthly payment and whether there are issues you'll need to address before closing.
- Getting preapproved early can pinpoint credit or account problems while there may still be time to fix them.
- Preapproval letters typically expire in 30 to 60 days, so time yours accordingly.
- In a fast-moving market, a strong preapproval letter can make your offer more competitive.

Questions to Ask First

Ask Your Lender

- ☐ Does the application fee include the credit report, or is that separate?
- ☐ Can you give me a closing cost estimate before I formally apply? You'll have a better idea of how much cash to have ready at closing.
- ☐ Can I get a preapproval letter before I start making offers?
- ☐ When can I lock in my interest rate and how long does that lock last?
- ☐ Does this loan come with any prepayment penalties?
- ☐ What's my full monthly payment, including taxes and insurance?
- ☐ What's the difference between my interest rate and my APR?
- ☐ Should I consider buying points to lower my rate?
- ☐ What loan options do I qualify for and why would I choose one over another?
- ☐ What could change between now and closing day?
- ☐ How long does this process usually take?

- ☐ Who will I be working with day to day and how quickly do they respond?
- ☐ What's the best way to send you documents?
- ☐ How much of this process can I handle online?
- ☐ What are the most common things that delay or kill a deal?
- ☐ How long have you been in the mortgage business?

Ask Yourself

- ☐ Do I know my credit score and how it impacts my loan options?
- ☐ Have I been preapproved or just prequalified?
- ☐ Is there anything in my financial history the lender might ask me to explain?

Warning Signs: Your Credit Readiness Checklist

Your credit report is going to play a major role in the mortgage approval process, so it's best to go into it prepared and educated. Here are some red flags to watch out for and address:

- ⊘ **Haven't pulled your credit report yet.** Get a free copy from all three bureaus at AnnualCreditReport.com before your lender does.
- ⊘ **Errors on your report that haven't been addressed.** Corrections take time. Fix them now, not when you're halfway into the mortgage application process.
- ⊘ **High balances on your credit cards.** How much you owe on your credit cards compared with your total credit limit can impact your score.
- ⊘ **Late payments in your recent history.** Payment history counts for about 35% of your FICO score, so late payments can pull your score down.
- ⊘ **Accounts in collections.** Unresolved debt can hold up an approval or change your loan terms.
- ⊘ **Applied for new credit recently.** Multiple inquiries in a short period can "ding" your score and make you look like a riskier bet.

- ⃠ **Unsure what credit score you need to qualify.** Ask your lender before you apply. You can also search online for some ranges to shoot for.
- ⃠ **Planning a big purchase before closing.** New debt can change your debt-to-income ratio and make lenders reconsider your approval.
- ⃠ **Paid off a debt recently but haven't checked your credit report.** It may take a month or two to update, so keep proof of payment in case your lender still sees the old balance.

Next Steps:
What the Underwriter Is Looking At

Underwriters are tough cookies, and it's their job to verify everything in your file. Here are some of the things they'll be looking for and expecting from you as you go through the mortgage approval process.

The 4 Cs of Credit

- **Capacity is your ability to repay.** Underwriters look at your income, how long you've earned it and how it compares to your monthly debt obligations.
- **Capital is your money.** The underwriters want to see that you can close and still have reserves left.
- **Collateral is the home itself.** The appraisal confirms that the property's value supports the loan amount.
- **Credit is your track record.** It shows how you've handled debt over time, including your score and payment history.

What to Expect

- Follow-up questions are normal. Answer them promptly and completely.
- Large deposits into your bank account may need to be explained.
- Paying off a debt while going through the application process can trigger a request for additional documentation.

- Nothing is personal. It's a risk review and everyone goes through it.
- Keep your financial life as predictable as possible between application and closing day.

If Your Credit Needs Work

- Pay on time, every time. Payment history makes up the largest share of your FICO score.
- Pay down credit card balances. High balances relative to your limit work against you.
- Stop applying for new credit while you're in the buying process.
- Deal with unpaid debt. A resolved account looks better than one that's still sitting out there ignored and unpaid.
- Changes don't happen overnight, so give the improvements a few billing cycles to show up on your report.

5 Questions Before You Move On

1) What do I know now that makes me feel more prepared than I was before?

2) What should I double-check right now before taking the next step?

3) What question do I need to ask my lender, agent, inspector, attorney or other professional?

4) What number, document, deadline or detail is keeping me up at night, and why?

5) What one thing should I confirm right now before moving on?

4

BUY A HOME THAT FITS YOUR LIFE

Smart Buyer Checklist: Single-Family vs. Townhouse vs. Condo

This is the point where everything starts to feel fun, fast and a little unhinged. You've educated yourself on the financing side, you probably have a price range in mind and now the listings are calling.

Before you start comparing properties, understand what you'll own, what you'll share and which repairs, fees and rules come with each housing type. Here's how single-family homes, townhouses, condos and co-ops differ.

Single-Family Home

- ☐ You own the house and the land under it.
- ☐ No shared walls, floors or ceilings.
- ☐ More privacy and more control over how you use the space.
- ☐ You handle all maintenance: lawn, roof, exterior and repairs.
- ☐ More room to renovate, expand or make the place your own.
- ☐ HOA rules may still apply depending on the neighborhood, so ask before you assume.
- ☐ Typically (but not always) the highest price point of the four options.

Townhouse

- ☐ Attached to neighboring units, usually sharing at least one wall.

- ☐ You typically own the unit and the land under it.
- ☐ More of a house feel than a condo, often with a private entrance, small yard or garage.
- ☐ Some exterior maintenance may be handled by the HOA.
- ☐ Before you buy, ask what you own, what the association controls and what your fees cover.
- ☐ Good middle ground if you want more space than a condo and less upkeep than a single-family home.

Condo

- ☐ You own the interior of your unit. The building and common areas are shared with other owners.
- ☐ Monthly association fees cover building maintenance, common areas and in some cases, amenities like a gym or pool.
- ☐ Less exterior upkeep, but more rules governing pets, rentals, parking, renovations and noise.
- ☐ Review the association's insurance policy carefully, since what it covers and what you're going to have to cover yourself are two different things.
- ☐ Check the reserve fund, any pending special assessments and recent meeting minutes before you buy.
- ☐ Do a quick Google News search on the building or community to see if anything unusual comes up.

Co-op

- ☐ You don't own the unit. You buy shares in a corporation that owns the entire building.
- ☐ Board approval is required before you can buy in, and they may ask for an interview.
- ☐ Monthly fees cover the building's mortgage, taxes, insurance and maintenance.
- ☐ More common in urban markets like New York, D.C. and Chicago than in suburban areas.
- ☐ Not all lenders offer share loans, so ask about financing options before you go too far down this road.

Reality Check

Before You Buy into HOA Communities

Homeowners association fees hit your account every month whether you love its rules and restrictions or not. Before you buy into any community with an HOA, use this checklist to make sure you can live with its rules and requirements.

- ☐ I know what the monthly fees are and exactly what they cover.
- ☐ I've looked at how often fees have increased and by how much.
- ☐ I know whether any special assessments are pending or have been discussed.
- ☐ I've reviewed the reserve fund and the HOA looks adequately funded.
- ☐ I've read the CC&Rs (covenants, conditions and restrictions) and understand what the association controls.
- ☐ The rules on pets, rentals, parking and exterior changes work for my life.

- ☐ I know what the association's insurance covers and what I need to cover.
- ☐ I've walked the property and talked to current owners, not just read the paperwork.
- ☐ I know who runs the association and how decisions get made.
- ☐ I've done a quick Google News search on the community.
- ☐ I know that HOA fees can increase, and I've left room for that in my budget.
- ☐ A well-run HOA can protect my property value, but one that's not can cost me money and time.

Questions to Ask: Co-Buying Checklist

Buying a home with a friend, sibling or longtime roommate can make homeownership possible when going solo isn't an option. Today's prices and rates have pushed a lot of buyers in this direction, and it can be a smart move.

Co-buying works best when the other person is reliable, your expectations are in sync and the arrangement is in writing before you close. Use these questions to figure out whether you've got the right person and the right plan.

About the Person

- ☐ How do they handle money day to day?
- ☐ Do they pay bills on time, consistently?
- ☐ Is their income stable enough to carry their share month after month?
- ☐ How do they handle conflict when something goes wrong or you disagree about money, repairs or the house?
- ☐ Do they want the same living setup and have the same expectations for the home?
- ☐ What would they do if they wanted out of the arrangement?

About the Arrangement

- ☐ How will you split the down payment, mortgage, taxes, insurance and repairs?
- ☐ What happens if one person wants to sell before the other does?
- ☐ How would a buyout work if one person wants out early?
- ☐ Who makes the final call on repairs and maintenance decisions?
- ☐ Can the home become a rental property if one owner moves out?
- ☐ If the home increases significantly in value, how will you split the financial gain?
- ☐ Was everything documented in a written agreement and reviewed by a real estate attorney?

About the Legal Setup

- ☐ Are you going with joint tenancy, which means equal shares, or tenancy in common, which allows a flexible ownership split?
- ☐ If ownership shares aren't equal, how do monthly expenses get split up and assigned?
- ☐ Does the agreement cover what happens if someone gets married, relocates or wants to buy a home of their own?
- ☐ Does your lender offer co-buyer financing, and have you talked through how both credit profiles affect the loan?

Warning Signs: 10 Things a Great Showing Can Hide

A showing is always going to present the best version of the property. These 10 warning signs can help you spot the parts that may become expensive, annoying or impossible to ignore once you live there.

1. **You hate yard work, but you're buying a single-family home with a large lot.** That lawn will still need to be cut every week, and those shrubs, trees and exterior won't take care of themselves.

2. **You're buying a condo, but haven't thought much about sharing elevators, hallways, walls and parking areas every day.** If close neighbors bother you as a renter, buying the unit won't make them less annoying.

3. **You're fine with the HOA rules but haven't read all of them.** Pay particular attention to any restrictions on pets, parking, rentals, renovations or guests.

4. **Parking is tight or nonexistent, and you're telling yourself it'll be fine**. Trust me, this is not a problem that gets easier to live with over time.

5. **You're buying with someone, but you haven't had the money conversation yet.** Decide who pays for what, how you'll split repairs and what happens if one of you wants out of the arrangement.

6. **You love the condo unit but haven't paid much attention to the building.** A beautiful, modern interior won't help much if the association has little money, major repairs coming or owners fighting over a special assessment.

7. **You're stretching your budget to afford a larger home when a smaller one would be more manageable right now.** The extra bedrooms also come with a higher payment, larger utility bills and more space to clean and maintain.

8. **The commute works on a good traffic day.** Drive it during your normal commute, not at 11 a.m. on a Saturday morning, before you make an offer.

9. **The building has deferred maintenance or very little money in reserves.** If the roof, elevators or other shared systems need major work, the owners may have to cover the bill through a special assessment.

10. **You're buying from your wish list instead of the life you live.** That wish list was fun to put together, but it doesn't pay your mortgage or sit in that rush hour commute every morning.

Next Steps: The Smaller-Home Tradeoff Checklist

A smaller home, condo or townhouse can get you into ownership sooner without overextending your finances. You may give up extra bedrooms, a larger yard or more privacy, but you could also get a lower payment, less upkeep and a better location. Here are eight signs that buying smaller now may work better than waiting for a larger or more expensive home.

- ☞ You want to start building equity now instead of waiting for home prices or interest rates to shift.
- ☞ The full monthly payment, including taxes, insurance, HOA fees and maintenance, fits your budget and leaves you money to spare.
- ☞ The location works for your commute, your priorities and the things you enjoy doing.
- ☞ You don't need a lot of space right now. Your first home doesn't have to solve every future need.
- ☞ Less upkeep sounds good to you. Fewer projects and a more manageable first year of ownership are the true benefits.
- ☞ You're open to a condo or townhouse, and the shared costs or lower price point make the tradeoff worthwhile.
- ☞ You have a realistic sense of how long you'll stay. A smaller place may work well for now, even if it doesn't fit your life forever.
- ☞ You're ready to stop renting and start owning, but you don't want to use up all your cash in the process.

5 Questions Before You Move On

1) What do I know now that makes me feel more prepared than I was before?

2) What should I double-check right now before taking the next step?

3) What question do I need to ask my lender, agent, inspector, attorney or other professional?

4) What number, document, deadline or detail is keeping me up at night, and why?

____

____

____

____

____

____

5) What one thing should I confirm right now before moving on?

____

____

____

____

____

____

5

LOOK BEYOND THE LISTING PHOTOS

Smart Buyer Checklist: What to Look for on Every Home Tour

The photos and virtual tours got you here, but the in-person showing is where you find out if the house fits your needs, preferences and lifestyle. Pull this checklist up and use it while you're walking through every house.

- [ ] Layout and flow. Does the floor plan fit your lifestyle, or does it just photograph well?
- [ ] Kitchen layout, counter space, storage and lighting.
- [ ] Bathrooms: condition, water pressure and ventilation.
- [ ] Bedroom size, closet space and natural light.
- [ ] Storage throughout: pantry, garage, attic or basement.
- [ ] Parking: driveway, garage and street. Is there enough of it?
- [ ] Yard and outdoor space: size, condition and the related upkeep.
- [ ] Natural light. Does it feel bright in there, or did the photographer use a lot of creative camera tricks?
- [ ] Noise: traffic, neighbors, the HVAC kicking on and anything else you'll hear every single day.

- ☐ The smell. Musty and moldy smelling areas—or rooms with a lot of air fresheners in them—should all get a second look.
- ☐ Floors: do they feel solid underfoot or do they bounce, sag or creak when you walk? (Some older homes with hardwood flooring are going to do this anyway, so factor the structure's age into your assessment.)
- ☐ Walls and ceilings: staining, cracks or anything that looks like old water damage whose root cause was never addressed.
- ☐ Doors and windows: do they open and close without a fight, or do they take all your strength?
- ☐ Age of the HVAC, water heater and electrical panel. These can all be expensive to fix, so be sure to ask about them.
- ☐ Cell service. Check it out on your phone while you're standing in the house.
- ☐ Work-from-home space, if that's part of your daily life.
- ☐ What's happening out on the street and next door, not just inside the home's front door.
- ☐ Your gut reaction to the house overall (write it down now, especially if you're touring multiple properties).

Reality Check

Online Listing Red Flags

Sellers and their agents are really good at making homes look their best before they hit the market, and that starts long before the listing photos are taken and virtual tours are created. But they can't hide everything. Here are some red flags to watch out for as you're scrolling.

- Beautifully furnished rooms followed by the same rooms completely empty. That's virtual staging. Judge the actual space when you walk through, not the digital version of it.
- Wide-angle lenses make rooms look bigger than they are. Some spaces will feel noticeably smaller once you're standing in them.
- Missing rooms or no exterior photos in the listing. Trust me, what's not shown is never an accident. If the primary bedroom is weirdly absent, or only makes a brief appearance, it's probably not the property's best selling point.
- "As-is," "investor special" or "priced to sell." Those phrases usually mean more work than the photos let on, but if you're into the DIY thing, by all means put them on your "maybe" list.

- "Cozy" almost always means small, and not always in a negative way. It's just the real estate agent's or owner's way of giving you the heads-up not to expect an expansive, sprawling space.
- A home that smells a little too good when you walk in. Again, fresh candles and air fresheners can cover a lot of things, including the mildew smell caused by water damage.
- A home that's been sitting with multiple price cuts. Ask your agent what's going on before you schedule a showing. The market itself could be creating the problem (e.g., the seller had high hopes, but the market had other ideas), but there also may be more to the story.
- No street or area shots in the listing. Most listings include neighborhood and aerial photos, but walk the block when you get there and see it for yourself.

Questions to Ask: Second Showing Checklist

You came back for a reason. It's time to go through each area of the home's interior and exterior carefully before you write an offer. You may have already tackled some of these on the first go-round, but just in case, here's a complete checklist to use on every second showing.

Exterior

- ☐ Are there signs of deferred maintenance: peeling paint, damaged siding or cracked walkways?
- ☐ Do the lines of the home look straight when you step back and look at it from the street?
- ☐ Does the roof sag? Walk across the street and look at it from a distance.
- ☐ Does the ground around the foundation slope toward the home or away from it?

Roof, Windows and Doors

- ☐ Are there curling, lifting or missing shingles?
- ☐ How old is the roof and when was it last replaced?
- ☐ Do windows open and close without sticking and is the caulking intact?
- ☐ Are there cracks in the drywall above door frames? That can be a sign of a settling foundation.

Inside the Home

- ☐ Do floors feel solid underfoot or do they bounce and sag in spots?
- ☐ Are walls and ceilings straight or do you see bowing, cracks or staining?
- ☐ Do doors and drawers open and close easily, or do they stick?
- ☐ Does the home smell right? If you detect a musty, moldy or chemical odor, ask about it.

Mechanical, Plumbing and Electrical

- ☐ How old are the HVAC system and water heater, and when were they last serviced?
- ☐ What do utilities run per month? Get real numbers, not guesses.
- ☐ Do all faucets, showers and tubs work and drain without issues?
- ☐ Has the electrical panel been updated? Older panels may not support a modern household's load.
- ☐ Are there enough outlets and are they well placed?

Everyday Livability

- ☐ How's the cell service inside? Check it before you leave.
- ☐ What internet providers serve the address and what are the available speeds? (You may need to investigate this one on your own, but most providers have online portals where you can plug in an address and see available plans).
- ☐ Is there a space that works as a home office if you need one?
- ☐ Are there any smart home systems, and which ones is the seller leaving with the property?

Warning Signs: Neighborhood and Investment Stability

The house might check every box, but the neighborhood is part of the investment too. Buy into an area where businesses are closing up shop and properties are neglected, and you may have a harder time selling it at a later date. Here are some early warning signs to watch for.

- ⦸ Multiple properties on the street look neglected or abandoned.
- ⦸ You see empty storefronts within a few blocks of the house.
- ⦸ You asked how long homes sit in this area and it sounds like they stagnate on the market.
- ⦸ The schools have low ratings and there's no sign of improvement.
- ⦸ Getting to a grocery store, doctor or highway takes longer than it should.
- ⦸ The parks and public spaces look like nobody's maintaining them.

- ⃠ Property taxes are higher than neighboring zip codes for no obvious reason.
- ⃠ The address is in a flood zone (and flood insurance isn't cheap).
- ⃠ New construction in the area looks like it has stopped or stalled out.
- ⃠ You're counting on future development that hasn't been approved or funded yet.
- ⃠ Crime stats for the area are higher than they are in surrounding neighborhoods.

Next Steps: Property-Needs-Work Decision Checklist

A house that needs work may have a lower asking price, but that doesn't make it a bargain. Before you fall for the fixer-upper, figure out what needs to be done, what it may cost and whether you can live with the disruption.

- ☐ Is the asking price around the same as similar homes nearby that are in better condition?
- ☐ Is the home structurally sound, or are there foundation, roof or water issues that go beyond cosmetic problems?
- ☐ How long has it been sitting on the market and why? Use Redfin or Zillow for the first answer, but you'll probably have to dig a little to get the "why?" answered.
- ☐ Can you get a contractor in the house before you make an offer, so you understand what you're taking on?
- ☐ Do you have a repair budget, with room left for surprises?
- ☐ Is there enough of a gap between the purchase price and the cost of repairs for the numbers to still make sense?
- ☐ Will you have enough cash reserves or other financial resources post-closing to handle the work?

- [ ] Are the problems cosmetic (paint, flooring or fixtures), or structural (foundation, roof, plumbing or electrical)? Some repairs can wait, but others may have to be handled before you can safely and comfortably live in the house.

- [ ] If you're buying as-is, do you understand what that means and that there are probably things that the seller just won't fix (even if the issues come up on your home inspection report)?

- [ ] Can you live there while the work is happening, or will you have to cover your mortgage and the cost of a temporary place at the same time?

- [ ] Does this home get you into a neighborhood or location you couldn't otherwise afford?

- [ ] Are your timelines realistic, or are you underestimating how long this is really going to take? It's always good to factor in some extra time because construction and remodeling projects are rarely completed on schedule.

5 Questions Before You Move On

1) What do I know now that makes me feel more prepared than I was before?

2) What should I double-check right now before taking the next step?

3) What question do I need to ask my lender, agent, inspector, attorney or other professional?

4) What number, document, deadline or detail is keeping me up at night, and why?

5) What one thing should I confirm right now before moving on?

6

BEFORE YOU COMMIT TO THE HOUSE

Smart Buyer Checklist: How Earnest Money Works

Earnest money is the deposit you put down when you make an offer to show the seller you're serious. It gets submitted with your purchase contract, goes into escrow and gets credited toward your down payment at closing. Here are some tips for deciding how much to put down.

- ☐ Standard earnest money runs 1% to 2% of the offer price in most markets. So that's $3,500 to $7,000 on a $350,000 home.
- ☐ Talk to your agent or attorney about what's customary in your market before writing a number down.
- ☐ In a competitive market with multiple offers, a larger deposit can make your offer stand out even if it isn't the highest one in the stack.
- ☐ In a slower market, a smaller deposit will usually do the job because you won't be getting into bidding wars with other buyers.
- ☐ Earnest money is generally refundable if the deal doesn't go through because of a contingency, like a failed inspection or loan denial.
- ☐ If you walk away from the deal without a contingency-based reason, you'll most likely lose your earnest money.
- ☐ Bottom line: Earnest money shows the seller you're serious, but it's also cash you could lose if you back out without a valid reason. Put down enough to make a good impression without overextending yourself.

Reality Check

Is Your Offer Based on Research or Vibes?

Do some homework before you put a number on paper. A house can feel right the minute you walk into it, but that feeling doesn't tell you the property's market value. Use this checklist to compare the asking price with recent sales, how long the home has been on the market and any price cuts. Then decide what you're willing to pay and write your offer.

- ☐ Focus on what comparable homes ("comps") have sold for, not just what they're listed at. There's usually a gap between those two numbers.
- ☐ Have your agent pull the comps and walk you through the data before you commit to a number.
- ☐ You can also do your own quick check by looking at similar homes that sold nearby in the last few months (not just homes that are listed for sale right now).
- ☐ Asking prices tell you what sellers want for their homes. Sold prices tell you what buyers paid.
- ☐ Make sure you're comparing homes that are similar: same square footage, age, condition, amenities, lot size and updates.

- ☐ Know the difference between what the comps support and what the seller is asking. If there's a big gap, factor that into your offer and your expectations.
- ☐ Pay attention to how long the home has been sitting on the market. A motivated seller may be more likely to negotiate with you.
- ☐ Excessive price reductions are a signal. Sometimes sellers aim high and then quickly correct, but others leave their homes on the market for months in hopes of snagging the right buyer. Find out how many reductions there have been and why.
- ☐ Never share the top of your budget (i.e., how high you're willing to go) with the seller's agent. They're not obligated to keep that information confidential, and it gives the seller an advantage before negotiations even start.

Questions to Ask:
Which Contingencies Should Be in Your Contract?

Contingencies are conditions that have to be met before the sale can close. If those conditions aren't met, you can usually walk away from the deal and get your earnest money back. Here are some contingencies you may want to include in your contract.

- ✓ **Financing.** Covers the loan amount, interest rate, term and a deadline for lender approval. This is an important contingency that protects your deposit if your mortgage doesn't come through.

- ✓ **Home inspection.** Gives you a set window to have the home inspected, and then ask for seller repairs, renegotiate or walk away if something major turns up.

- ✓ **Appraisal**. Protects you if the home appraises for less than your offer price. Your lender bases the loan on the appraised value, not the price you agreed to pay. If the appraisal comes in low, this contingency may give you room to renegotiate, bring more cash to closing or walk away without losing your deposit.

- ✓ **Clear title.** The seller has to prove they own the property free of liens or other claims before the deal can close.

- ✓ **Sale of current home.** This protects your deposit if you need to sell another home before you can buy. Sellers don't always love this contingency, but it's both common and workable.

- ✓ **HOA document review.** Gives you time to review the association's financials, rules, reserves and any pending assessments before you're locked in.
- ✓ **Homeowners insurance.** This one lets you walk away from the deal if you can't get coverage at a price that makes the deal work.
- ✓ **Radon or mold inspection.** If the home has a basement, a history of water issues or any signs of moisture damage, you'll want to include this one in your contract.
- ✓ **Septic and well.** This contingency is fairly standard on rural properties.
- ✓ **Job or relocation**. If you're moving for a position that isn't officially confirmed yet, this protects your deposit until the employment paperwork is signed.

Warning Signs to Watch For: Deal Breakers Before You Sign

A house can lose its appeal pretty quickly once the repairs, insurance costs or contract risks start adding up. Check these warning signs before you sign anything, drop a contingency or make an offer on a house you already know has costly problems.

- ⃠ The seller wants you to waive your inspection, financing, appraisal or insurance protections.
- ⃠ The home has been sitting on the market longer than similar homes nearby.
- ⃠ The seller has cut the price multiple times within a short period of time.
- ⃠ The seller pushes back on inspections or repair questions.
- ⃠ The house needs repairs you can't afford right away.
- ⃠ The monthly payment is already starting to make you nervous.
- ⃠ The insurance quote comes in higher than expected.
- ⃠ The home has an older roof, flood risk, past claims or known regional risks (e.g., hurricane, tornado or wildfire exposure).
- ⃠ You're cutting the numbers too close. If a single repair, insurance increase, tax change or closing cost surprise would put you in a financial bind, pause before making an offer.
- ⃠ Your gut says something feels off, but you're trying to ignore it because you want the house.

Next Steps: Check Insurance Before You Write the Offer

Don't wait until you're under contract to find out what the home will cost to insure. A high premium, old roof, flood risk or past claim could add hundreds to your monthly costs, or leave you struggling to find coverage at all. Ask these questions before you write the offer.

- ☐ **What does the current owner pay for homeowners insurance?** It won't be your exact number, but it gives you a starting point to work from.

- ☐ **Has a claim ever been filed on the home?** A history of water or wind damage can affect your premiums or make it difficult to get coverage at all.

- ☐ **Is the home in a flood zone?** Flood insurance is sold separately from homeowners insurance and can add significant cost to your monthly budget.

- ☐ **How old is the roof?** In some states, a roof that's over 15 years old can disqualify you from coverage with certain carriers.

- ☐ **Are there regional risks to factor in?** Hurricanes, tornadoes, wildfires and earthquakes all come with their own insurance risks.

- ☐ **Get at least one insurance quote before committing.** If you can't get coverage at a price that makes the deal work, it's much better to know that information ahead of time (and not at closing).

5 Questions Before You Move On

1) What do I know now that makes me feel more prepared than I was before?

2) What should I double-check right now before taking the next step?

3) What question do I need to ask my lender, agent, inspector, attorney or other professional?

4) What number, document, deadline or detail is keeping me up at night, and why?

5) What one thing should I confirm right now before moving on?

7

STAY ON TOP OF INSPECTIONS, TITLE & DISCLOSURES

Smart Buyer Checklist: How to Read Your Inspection Report

The inspection report will probably be long and detailed. Use this checklist to see what the inspector reviewed and flag anything you need to ask about before you go any further.

Structure and Exterior

☐ Foundation condition

☐ Floor structure and exterior walls

☐ Roof structure, covering, flashing and gutters

☐ Siding, trim, soffits and fascia

Grounds and Access

☐ Driveway, walkways and porches

☐ Garage, garage doors and exterior doors

☐ Windows: condition, operation and sealing

Interior

☐ Interior doors, walls and ceilings

☐ Floors throughout

☐ Basement or crawl space

☐ Attic, insulation and ventilation

Electrical

- ☐ Electrical panel and any subpanels
- ☐ Grounding, wiring type and outlets
- ☐ Smoke detectors

Mechanical and Plumbing

- ☐ Heating and cooling systems and ductwork
- ☐ Water heater and location of main water shutoff
- ☐ Visible supply and drain lines

Other

- ☐ Appliances that are included in the sale
- ☐ Signs of moisture or drainage problems anywhere in the home
- ☐ Safety concerns flagged by the inspector
- ☐ Items the inspector recommends sending to a specialist (follow up on all of these)

Reality Check: Defect Decision Guide

If your contract includes an inspection contingency, you can ask for repairs, request a credit or walk away from the deal. If the seller won't budge on serious, expensive issues—and if the numbers no longer work—you can cancel the contract. Use this guide to separate manageable fixes from potentially costly problems.

- **Major structural problems**: foundation cracks, roof damage, framing issues. Get a specialist to inspect before you make a final decision.
- **Failing or end-of-life systems:** HVAC, water heater, electrical panel. Factor replacement costs into the negotiation or ask for a credit at closing.
- **Water intrusion or mold:** Don't assume it's minor and manageable. Get a specialist and find out the root cause before you go any further.
- **Safety issues:** Unsafe wiring, missing smoke detectors, code violations. You can definitely ask the seller to handle these before closing.
- **Items flagged for specialist review:** The inspector flagged them for a reason, so don't skip the follow-up.
- **Cosmetic issues:** Paint, minor cracks, dated fixtures. If it looks like something you can deal with after closing, it may not be worth negotiating over.

Questions to Ask: As-Is Property Gut Check

When a seller lists a home as-is, they're telling you upfront they won't fix anything. You can still inspect it, but you can't expect them to jump into action repairing the problems that the inspector finds. Review these questions before you commit to an as-is property.

- ☐ Do you understand what as-is means? It's not a discount or a fixer-upper deal. With these deals, the seller has decided that they don't want to fix anything, period.
- ☐ Have you scheduled a full inspection? You can and should get one, but you just won't have much (or any, in some cases) leverage to negotiate repairs afterward.
- ☐ Have you obtained contractor estimates for the visible problems? Get some real numbers before you make an offer.
- ☐ Does the asking price reflect the true condition? As-is homes may sell for less than comparable properties that are in better shape.
- ☐ Do you have enough cash after closing to handle repairs without overtaxing your budget? There are always going to be things that come up after closing, so have some reserves to cover them.
- ☐ Have you read the seller disclosure carefully? They still have to disclose known defects on an as-is sale.
- ☐ Do you have an inspection contingency in the contract? Without one, you'll have to deal with whatever comes up on the report yourself.

Warning Signs to Watch For: Title, Disclosure & Insurance Issues

On the Seller Disclosure

- ⃠ Blank spaces where there should be answers. Sellers can say they don't know, but leaving questions unanswered is a different story. Ask your agent to follow up.
- ⃠ A history of water damage, flooding or pest infestations. Find out what was done about it and when.
- ⃠ Roof leaks or HVAC problems that were disclosed but not repaired. Get documentation of any prior work.
- ⃠ Structural work or renovations done without permits. Unpermitted work becomes your problem as soon as you take ownership.
- ⃠ Flood zone status that wasn't mentioned upfront. That could require a separate flood insurance policy and a higher monthly housing cost.
- ⃠ Undisclosed, open HOA assessments. These financial obligations will transfer with the property and become your problem.

On the Title Report

- ⃠ Unpaid liens or judgments against the property.
- ⃠ Past-due property taxes.
- ⃠ Gaps or disputes in the ownership history.
- ⃠ Easements that affect how you can use the property.
- ⃠ Any issue the title company says must be resolved before closing.

On the Title Insurance Policy

- ⃠ Your lender's title policy protects the lender.
- ⃠ An owner's title policy protects your interest in the home.
- ⃠ Both are typically a one-time premium paid at closing.
- ⃠ Ask what's excluded from the coverage before you sign anything.

Next Steps: How to Stay Sane During the Closing Countdown

The stretch between signed contract and closing day can be stressful. You've done the hard work and now you're in a waiting game, where everything feels urgent and the deal seems to be taking forever to close. Here's how to get through it.

- **Manage what you can control.** Start packing, research movers, set up utilities at the new place and start your address change notifications. Staying busy with productive tasks can help take your mind off the waiting game.
- **Send your lender each document as soon as they ask for it.** Waiting too long can delay underwriting and push back your closing date.
- **Give yourself one check-in window per day.** Look at your email, follow up with your agent if needed and then put the phone down. Refreshing your inbox every few minutes won't move the closing date.
- **Stay off the mortgage rate rabbit holes and real estate horror story forums.** They'll only add to your anxiety. If you need facts or reassurance, talk to your lender, mortgage broker or real estate agent about your concerns. Even though every transaction is unique, there's probably nothing you can ask or tell them that they haven't heard before.

☞ **Talk to a homeowner who's been through this before.** Sometimes you just need someone to tell you that the waiting, second-guessing and last-minute requests are normal.

☞ **Don't make any big financial moves while you're waiting.** I like to call this my "financial austerity" phase: no new credit, no large purchases, no job changes. Keep your financial life as consistent as possible until the keys are in your hand.

☞ **When the Closing Disclosure arrives, compare it carefully to your original Loan Estimate.** Flag anything that changed and ask your lender for an explanation.

☞ **And ask your agent for a quick weekly update** so you're not just sitting there, wondering what's happening and dreaming up worst-case scenarios.

5 Questions Before You Move On

1) What do I know now that makes me feel more prepared than I was before?

2) What should I double-check right now before taking the next step?

3) What question do I need to ask my lender, agent, inspector, attorney or other professional?

4) What number, document, deadline or detail is keeping me up at night, and why?

____
____
____
____
____
____

5) What one thing should I confirm right now before moving on?

____
____
____
____
____
____

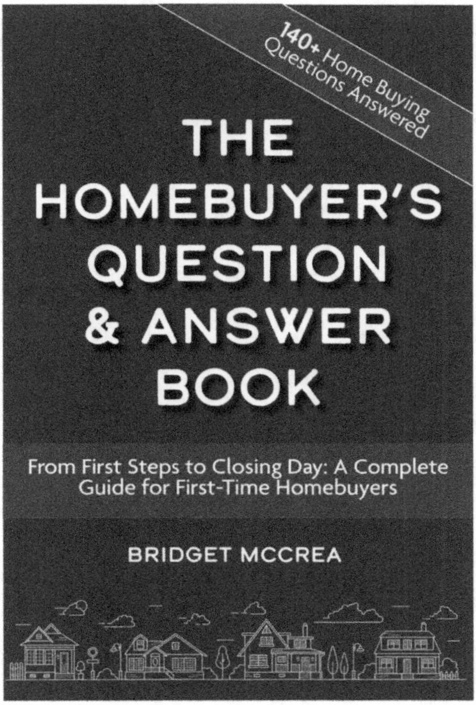

Would You Rather Have All the Answers in One Place?

If you're already well into the homebuying process and need the full picture in one place, *The Homebuyer's Question & Answer Book* walks you through the journey from first steps to closing day. It's the anchor book in this First-Time Homebuyer Series and a great resource to keep nearby if your purchase has extra moving parts, tight deadlines or questions coming at you faster than expected.

8

WALK INTO CLOSING PREPARED, WALK OUT A HOMEOWNER

Smart Buyer Checklist: How to Read Your Closing Disclosure

Your lender will send the Closing Disclosure at least three business days before your actual closing date. When you get it, compare it to your original Loan Estimate and make sure everything still looks right. If something changed, ask your lender to explain it before closing day. Here are some of the key items to review.

☐ Property address, buyer and seller names, loan type, loan amount, interest rate, loan term and closing date.

☐ Projected monthly payment, including principal, interest, taxes, insurance and escrow.

☐ Cash-to-close amount, including your down payment, closing costs and any credits.

☐ Lender fees: origination, underwriting, points and credit report charges.

☐ Third-party fees: appraisal, title search, title insurance, settlement and recording charges.

☐ Prepaid taxes, homeowners insurance and prepaid interest.

☐ Escrow deposits for future taxes and insurance.

☐ Prorated taxes, HOA dues or other costs split between buyer and seller.

- [ ] Seller credits, lender credits and your earnest money deposit credit.

- [ ] Final loan calculations, total closing costs and total amount financed.

- [ ] Anything that looks different from your Loan Estimate. Your lender can walk you through any changes before closing day, so there are no surprises at the table.

Reality Check: Your Final Walk-Through Checklist

The final walk-through is one of the best parts of the whole process. The house is empty, it's almost yours and you get to walk through it one last time before you sign. Use this list to make sure the seller didn't leave behind damage, missing items or unfinished repairs.

- ☐ Every appliance included in the sale is still there and working.
- ☐ Heating and cooling systems are operational.
- ☐ All faucets, toilets and water fixtures work, and there are no leaks or water pressure issues.
- ☐ The sellers didn't damage any walls, floors or door frames on their way out.
- ☐ Everything the contract said stays is still there.
- ☐ All agreed-upon repairs were completed and look like they were handled properly.
- ☐ The home is in the same general condition it was when you made the offer.
- ☐ The seller has fully moved out.
- ☐ You've checked the garage, attic, basement and any outbuildings.
- ☐ If anything looks off, point it out to your agent during the walk-through so it can be addressed before closing.

Questions to Ask: What Should You Bring to Closing?

A few days before closing, confirm the date, time, location and final cash-to-close amount with your closing agent. That person should also tell you exactly what to bring to closing, but use this list as a backup.

- ☐ A government-issued photo ID: driver's license, passport or military ID.
- ☐ A cashier's check or wire confirmation for your closing funds. Confirm the exact amount and delivery method ahead of time.
- ☐ Proof of homeowners insurance, if your lender or closing agent asks for it.
- ☐ Your fully charged phone, since you may need email access, wire confirmation details and/or digital documents at the table.
- ☐ Any receipts for closing-related expenses you already paid, like inspection or appraisal fees.
- ☐ Any documents your lender, title company, attorney or closing agent specifically asked you to bring.
- ☐ Your co-borrower or spouse, if that person also has to sign.
- ☐ Wiring instructions confirmed directly by phone with your title company before you send anything.

Warning Signs to Watch For: A Few Things to Know Before You Close

- **Wire fraudsters target real estate transactions, so confirm before you send funds.** If you get an email with updated wiring instructions, call your title company directly—using a number you looked up yourself—before moving any money.
- **Your lender does a final check on your finances before closing.** Keep things consistent between contract and closing, so no new credit, big purchases or job changes during this time.
- **Numbers on the Closing Disclosure may look a little different from what you saw on the Loan Estimate.** Some variation is normal, but ask for an explanation if anything changed more than you expected.
- **The seller asks to stay in the home after closing.** This is uncommon, but it does happen. Don't agree unless the move-out date, payment, security deposit and responsibility for damage are all in writing.
- **Closing dates occasionally shift by a day or two.** Closing day is set well in advance, but moving it up or back a day or two is fairly common. Don't freak out if yours changes because of a lender delay, title issue, document problem, final walk-through concern or scheduling conflict.

Next Steps: Your New Homeowner Document Tracker

It's time to organize your new home paperwork. Future you will be thankful when something needs attention, and you know exactly where everything is.

Take These with You from the Closing Table

A lot of closing paperwork is digital now, but you still need to save copies in one place. Before you walk out of the closing appointment, ask which documents you'll receive that day, which ones will come later and where you can access the full closing package.

- ☐ Closing Disclosure
- ☐ Promissory note and mortgage or deed of trust
- ☐ Copy of the deed, if provided at closing (the recorded deed may come later)
- ☐ Title insurance documents, including lender and owner policies
- ☐ Purchase contract and any addenda or amendments
- ☐ Seller disclosure and any repair or credit agreements associated with the sale
- ☐ Survey and appraisal, if you received copies
- ☐ First mortgage payment instructions, including the due date, amount due and where to send it

Hold Onto These Docs

- ☐ Monthly mortgage statements
- ☐ Property tax bills and any homestead exemption filings
- ☐ Homeowners insurance policy and renewal notices
- ☐ HOA documents, fee schedules and meeting minutes, if applicable
- ☐ Receipts for home-related repairs, renovations and major purchases
- ☐ Permits for any work done on the property
- ☐ Appliance manuals and warranties
- ☐ Contractor names, invoices and contact information
- ☐ Before-and-after photos of any larger projects
- ☐ Your annual IRS Form 1098 from your lender (which shows mortgage interest paid)

Tips for Keeping It Simple

- ☐ Create one main folder, binder or digital drive for everything related to the house
- ☐ Break the folder into categories: mortgage, insurance, taxes, repairs, warranties and utilities
- ☐ Scan receipts and warranties with your phone as soon as you get them
- ☐ Take photos of serial numbers, paint labels, flooring samples and appliance model numbers
- ☐ Set calendar reminders for insurance renewals, HVAC service and property tax deadlines
- ☐ Go back through the folder every couple of months so it stays current and useful

5 Questions Before You Move On

1) What do I know now that makes me feel more prepared than I was before?

____

____

____

____

____

____

2) What should I double-check right now before taking the next step?

____

____

____

____

____

____

3) What question do I need to ask my lender, agent, inspector, attorney or other professional?

____

____

____

____

____

____

4) What number, document, deadline or detail is keeping me up at night, and why?

5) What one thing should I confirm right now before moving on?

KEEP THIS BOOK HANDY UNTIL THE KEYS ARE YOURS

You made it through all eight chapters, which means you now know more than many buyers do when they start searching online, touring homes or filling out a loan application. You know what happens next, where the expensive mistakes tend to happen and which questions to ask before you sign anything. Knowing what to watch for won't prevent every surprise, but it will help you slow down, ask better questions and avoid being rushed into a bad decision.

Keep this book nearby through closing and your first year as a homeowner. Go back to the document tracker in Chapter Eight, along with any notes, questions and reminders you added as you worked through the book. You'll need some of that information again when the first tax bill arrives, an insurance question comes up or something in the house needs attention.

Before you close the book, grab your free *First-Time Homebuyer's Home Tour Toolkit* on the next page. It includes three quick checklists you can save to your phone and use during tours, second visits and those moments when you're standing in the driveway wondering whether anyone checked the roof, water heater or electrical panel.

If this book helped you, please leave a quick Amazon review. You can also share it with a friend who's thinking about buying or send it to someone who's already deep into the search and starting to feel overwhelmed. A short review can help another buyer find the answers they need before they start making offers.

You've got this. Go get those keys.

Bridget McCrea

GET YOUR FREE HOMEBUYER TOOLKIT

Before you close this book, grab a free PDF you can keep on your phone and bring to every showing. *The First-Time Homebuyer's Home Tour Toolkit* includes three checklists pulled directly from this book:

- ☑ **The Ultimate Home Tour Checklist** — everything to look for the first time through, from location to layout to the details most buyers breeze past.
- ☑ **The Second Showing Checklist** — a room-by-room checklist to run through before you make an offer.
- ☑ **Six Red Flags to Watch For** — the warning signs that good staging, great photos and first-walkthrough excitement hide so well.

It's free and takes 30 seconds.

Scan the code below or visit strongtide-toolkit.subscribepage.io

PAY IT FORWARD FOR THE BUYER STARTING WHERE YOU DID

Buying your first home is one of the most overwhelming things you'll ever do, and I know that firsthand. If ***I'm Buying My First Home. Now What?*** helped you navigate the process, understand what you were signing or just feel a little less alone in all of this, would you take a minute to share that in a short Amazon review?

Even just a few words can encourage the next first-time buyer who's stressed, confused and wondering if they can pull this off. Reviews help others find the book and take the first step toward owning their own home.

Every review adds to a growing community of first-time buyers who figured it out and paid it forward. I'd love for you to be part of it.

BUILD ON WHAT YOU'VE LEARNED HERE

Want the full explanation behind the checklists in this book? Your next read is ***The Homebuyer's Question & Answer Book***. It answers more than 140 questions about the numbers, choices and decisions that come up from first steps to closing day.

For worksheets, comparison pages and planning space, ***The First-Time Homebuyer Roadmap*** is the companion workbook for financing, comparing properties and getting to the closing table. Start with the book that matches where you are, then come back to this one whenever you need a quick refresh or gut check.

Coming soon: ***The First-Year Homeowner Handbook*** and ***The New Homeowner's Companion*** for everything that happens after you move in.

These are the books I wish I'd had when I was sitting where you are right now. Follow me on Amazon and be the first to know when the next one drops.

ABOUT THE AUTHOR

First of all, much gratitude for allowing me to play a small role in your homebuying journey. Know that I do not take that trust and responsibility lightly.

I'm Bridget McCrea. I've hustled through dead-end jobs, stretched a bank account that was almost empty, raised a toddler while chasing deadlines and built a business with nothing but determination, a desktop and a Texas Instruments 1200-baud modem at my kitchen table.

Real estate found me early and never really let go:

1) Right out of college, I started as a Century 21 agent when the MLS was a thick, physical book filled with basic home details and one black-and-white exterior photo per listing. My stint as an agent was short-lived, but I learned the inner workings of an industry that's a mysterious black box for many.

2) Writing for publications like Inman News and REALTOR Magazine, I had a front-row seat when IDX launched and

changed everything. For the first time, buyers could see homes, photos, virtual tours and property details online without going through an agent first.

3) Being asked to write *Second Homes for Dummies* (Wiley & Co.) and *The RE/MAX Home Buyer's Survival Guide* (Sterling Publishing) pulled me even deeper into the industry and led to an AMACOM series that included *The Real Estate Agent's Business Planner* and *The Homebuyer's Question & Answer Book*, which I recently updated for a new generation of first-time homebuyers.

Across all of these projects, my goal never changes: give readers the information they need to make smarter money, life and business decisions. I've also been in your shoes a few times—and most recently as a divorced, self-employed woman, which doesn't exactly make lenders jump for joy—so I know how it feels when your own money, credit history, inspection report and closing date are on the line.

You've got this, and now you've got this first-time homebuyer book series in your corner. Go get 'em.

StrongTide Press Books

Practical guidebooks for big decisions, expensive moments and the questions that come with them.

FIRST-TIME HOMEBUYER SERIES

The Homebuyer's Question & Answer Book

From First Steps to Closing Day: A Complete Guide for First-Time Homebuyers

I'm Buying My First Home. Now What?

A Roadmap from First Search to Closing Day

The First-Time Homebuyer Roadmap

A Workbook for Financing, Comparing Properties and Getting to the Closing Table

***Coming Soon:* The First-Year Homeowner Handbook**

A Step-by-Step Guide to the Decisions, Details and To-Dos Ahead

***Coming Soon:* The New Homeowner's Companion**

A Guided Planner for Your First Year, From Move-In to Settled In

FOR AGENTS & BROKERS

The Real Estate Agent's Business Planner

The Proven System for Generating Leads, Winning Clients and Building a Profitable Real Estate Career

The Real Estate Agent's 12-Month Planning Workbook

The Month-by-Month Planner for Managing Leads, Clients, Income, and Results

FOR FOUNDERS

Your First Business Blueprint

How to Plan, Launch and Grow a Profitable Small Business

The Business Money Blueprint

How to Fund Your Business From Self-Funding to Investor Capital

The Small Business Growth Blueprint

How to Grow Your Business by Turning Customers Into Lifelong Fans

Blueprints Beat Cocktail Napkins

How to Create a Winning Business Plan for Growth and Profit

www.ingramcontent.com/pod-product-compliance
Lightning Source LLC
LaVergne TN
LVHW022100200926
848481LV00003B/1005